520771920

MW00845516

DESIGNS IN SCIENCE

USING ENERGY

SALLY and ADRIAN MORGAN

Using Energy
Copyright © 1993 by Evans Brothers Limited

Facts On File, Inc.
460 Park Avenue South
New York NY 10016

Library of Congress Cataloging-in Publication-Data
Morgan, Sally.
    Using energy / Sally Morgan, Adrian Morgan.
    p. cm — (Designs in science)
    Includes index.
    Summary: Discusses the basic principles of energy and describes how it is extracted form its sources and put to use within the natural context and in human invention.
        ISBN 0–8160–2984–9
        1. Force and energy—Juvenile literature. 2. Power resources—Juvenile literature. 3. Heating—Juvenile literature. 4 Cooling—Juvenile literature. [1. Force and energy. 2. Power resources. 3. Heat.] I. Morgan, Adrian. II. Title. III. Series. IV. Series: Morgan, Sally. Designs in science.
QC73.4.M67 1993   93-20407
531' .6—dc20

Printed by Wing King Tong Co Ltd.

Managing Editor: Su Swallow
Editor: Catherine Bradley
Designer: Neil Sayer
Production: Peter Thompson
Illustrations: Hardlines, Charlbury

Acknowledgments

For permission to reproduce copyright material the authors and publishers gratefully acknowledge the following:

Cover Martin Bond, Science Photo Library
Title page Science Photo Library
Contents page Sally Morgan, Ecoscene **page 6** (top) Dr Vic Bradbury, Science Photo Library (bottom) Dr Gary Settles and Stephen McIntyre, Science Photo Library **page 7** Tony Craddock, Science Photo Library **page 8** (top) NASA, Science Photo Library (bottom) Geoff Williams, Science Photo Library **page 9** Gryniewiccz, Ecoscene **page 10** (top) NASA, Science Photo Library (bottom) Tom Bieber Inc, The Image Bank **page 11** Sally Morgan, Ecoscene **page 12** (top) Peter Scoones, Planet Earth Pictures (bottom left) Wendy Shattil and Bob Rozinski, Oxford Scientific Films (bottom right) Robert Harding Picture Library **page 13** (top) Whittle, Ecoscene (bottom) Sally Morgan, Ecoscene **page 14** (top) Sally Morgan, Ecoscene (middle) Doug Allan, Oxford Scientific Films (bottom) Martin Bond, Science Photo Library **page 15** K.H. Switak, NHPA **page 16** (top) Sally Morgan, Ecoscene (bottom) Ocean Images Inc, The Image Bank **page 18** (top) Towse, Ecoscene (bottom) Sheila Terry, Robert Harding Picture Library **page 19** Anthony Bannister, NHPA **page 20** (top) Photri, Robert Harding Picture Library (bottom) Sally Morgan, Ecoscene **page 21** (left) Ecoscene (right) Groves, Ecoscene **page 22** (top) Philippe Plailly, Science Photo Library (middle and bottom) Sally Morgan, Ecoscene **page 23** Dannett, Ecoscene **page 24** (top) Wilkinson, Ecoscene (bottom) Sheila Terry, Robert Harding Picture Library **page 25** Tony Craddock, Science Photo Library **page 26** John Farmar, Ecoscene **page 27** (top) Adam Hart-Davis, Science Photo Library (bottom) Sally Morgan, Ecoscene **page 28** (top) Simon Fraser, Science Photo Library (bottom left) US Dept of Energy, Science Photo LIbrary (bottom right) John Mead, Science Photo Library **page 29** Lowell Georgia, Science Photo Library **page 30** Sally Morgan, Ecoscene **page 31** (top) Jane Burton, Bruce Coleman Limited (bottom) A.N.T. (Dave Watts), NHPA **page 32** (left) David Parker, Science Photo Library (right) Sally Morgan, Ecoscene **page 33** G & P Corrigan, Robert Harding Picture Library **page 32** (top) Bildagentur Schuster/ Kuchlbauer, Robert Harding Picture Library (bottom) Will & Demi McIntyre, Science Photo Library **page 34** Harwood, Ecoscene **page 35** (top) Sally Morgan, Ecoscene (bottom) Terry Heathcote, Oxford Scientific Films **page 36** (left) George Bernard, NHPA (right) Seth Joel, Science Photo Library **page 37** (top) Stephen Dalton, NHPA (bottom) Sally Morgan, Ecoscene **page 39** Kim Hart, Robert Harding Picture Library **page 40** (top) John P Kelly, The Image Bank (bottom) Thomas Buchholz, Bruce Coleman Limited **page 41** Peter Grumann, The Image Bank **page 42** (top) Sally Morgan, Ecoscene (middle) Gerard Vandstadt, Agence Vandstadt (bottom) London Scientific Films/Oxford Scientific Films **page 44** (top) Gazidis, Ecoscene (middle) Martin Bond, Science Photo Library (bottom) Lawrence Livermore, National Laboratory/University of California, Science Photo Library **page 45** Hans Reinhard, Bruce Coleman Limited

DESIGNS IN SCIENCE
USING ENERGY

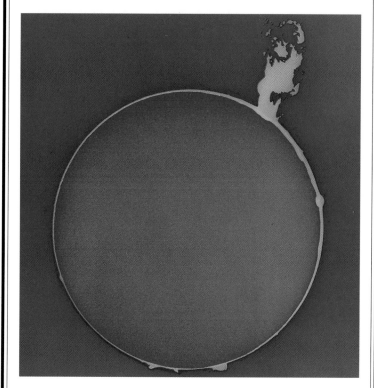

SALLY and ADRIAN MORGAN

Facts On File

NOTE ON MEASUREMENTS:

In this book, we have provided U.S. equivalents
for metric measurements when appropriate for
readers who are more familiar with these units.
However, as most scientific formulas are
calculated in metric units, metric units are given
first and are used alone in formulas.

Measurement

These abbreviations are used in this book.

METRIC		U.S. EQUIVALENT	
		Units of energy	
J	joule	**J**	joule
kJ	kilojoule	**Cal.**	Calorie
		Unit of force	
N	Newton	**N**	Newton
		Units of electric energy	
V	volt	**V**	volt
mV	millivolt	**mV**	millivolt
A	ampere	**A**	ampere
		Units of mass	
g	grame	**oz.**	ounces
		Units of length	
km	kilometer	**mi.**	mile
cm	centimeter	**in.**	inch
		Units of temperature	
°C	degrees Celsius	**°F**	degrees Fahrenheit

Using Energy is one book in the seven-volume series
Designs in Science. The series is designed to develop young
people's knowledge and understanding of the basic
principles of movement, structures, energy, light, sound,
materials and water, using an integrated science approach.
A central theme running through the series is the close link
between design in the natural world and design in modern
technology.

Contents

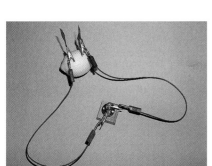

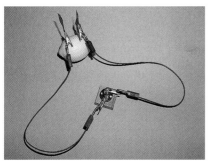

Lightning is an example of natural electric energy, produced by the build-up of electric charges in the atmosphere.

Moving objects possess kinetic energy. At the time of impact, the kinetic energy of the bullet is transferred to the egg, causing it to explode.

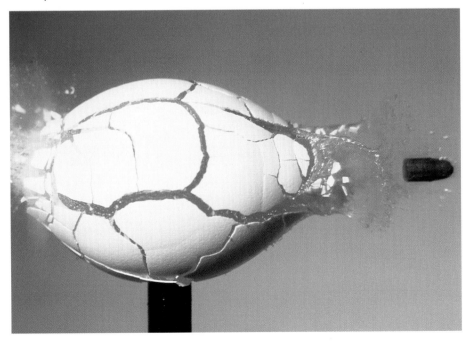

Introduction

All life needs energy. Our bodies need it to move, to breathe and to reproduce. Energy is also needed to make machines work, to cook with and to heat homes. It is difficult to describe what energy is, but it is quite easy to say what it does: Energy can do work. It can apply forces and move things. It can also heat things so that they melt, boil or evaporate. There are many forms of energy. Chemical energy, electric energy, movement energy and heat energy are all different forms of the same thing.

Energy is not made of atoms so it cannot be touched. Energy is concerned with the way molecules are arranged. Consider an elastic band. When a force is applied to stretch the band, the molecules within the elastic are pulled further apart. When the force is removed and the band released, the molecules return to their original positions. As this happens, the elastic band itself is able to do some work. For example, the elastic band could be part of a catapult. Work is first put into pulling the elastic band backward. This work is stored as potential energy. This energy is ready to be used to do something. The stored energy is converted to movement, or kinetic energy, when the band is released. The force that is produced can be enough to hurl a stone forward. If the moving stone hits a window, it can transfer its energy to the glass and cause it to break. The further the band is stretched, the more potential energy that can be stored, and the greater the amount of work the band can do when the band is released. If the band is not stretched enough, the amount of stored energy will be too small to do anything useful.

Work is really a transfer of energy. The moving object obtains its energy from whatever produces the force. The energy given to the moving object can be used to do work.

Transforming energy

There is a very important law in physics that states that energy can neither be created nor destroyed. However, energy can be changed from one form to another. It is said to have been "transformed." Although the amount of energy before the transformation is always the same as the amount after it, the quality or type of energy changes. Each energy conversion produces some heat energy that can be useful to living organisms. But this heat is often useless in human-made machines and contributes to warming up the atmosphere. So the amount of usable energy decreases as a result of transformation — it has been degraded.

Although energy cannot be touched, it can be measured in units called joules or in units called calories. On many packages of food there are numbers that indicate how much chemical energy is contained in that particular food. The number will be given in Calories (the capital C indicates that this means kilocalories, or 1,000 calories).

The ultimate source of most of the energy on the earth is the sun. The energy comes from billions of nuclear reactions that are taking place constantly in the very center of the sun. In fact, the sun can be thought of as a huge, natural, nuclear reactor. However, the sun is not a limitless source of energy. It is losing mass at a rate of 4 million tonnes (4,400,000 tons) per second. One day, millions of years from now, it will stop shining altogether.

This book examines how energy can be captured, converted, conserved and used in human-made machines. It also looks at the way living organisms, including people, use energy in their everyday lives. Important words are explained under the heading of **Key words** and in the glossary on page 46. You will find some amazing facts in each section together with some experiments for you to try and some questions for you to think about.

Food contains chemical energy that is released when the food is eaten. This energy is converted to another form of energy in our bodies.

A 16-year-old girl needs to eat about 9 million joules (2,150 Cal.) of energy every day and a 16-year-old boy needs 12 million joules (2,866 Cal.).

Heat energy

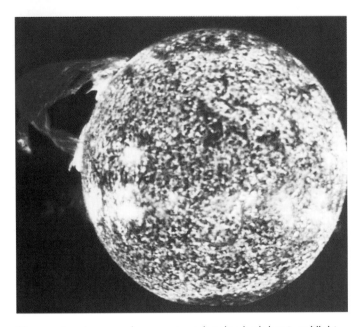

The sun is a huge nuclear reactor releasing both heat and light energy.

The sun is the source of most of our heat. At the center of the sun, temperatures may exceed 14,000,000°C (25,200,000°F). Even at the surface of the sun, the temperature is still 6,000°C (10,832°F).

Heat is created by moving molecules. The faster that molecules move or vibrate within a substance, the hotter the substance becomes. The temperature of an object tells us how hot it is. So temperature is really a measure of how fast the molecules are moving.

Heat can be transferred in many ways. As something becomes warmer, its heat is passed to its surroundings so that the surroundings warm up. When you stand on a cold surface, such as a stone floor, you lose heat energy to the floor and your feet feel cold. This is caused by conduction. A radiator produces warm air that you can feel if you put your hand above the radiator. The heat that your hand feels is a result of billions of fast-moving air molecules. The heat from the radiator is spread by convection. Heat can also be transferred by radiation, like the heat from the sun and from an open fire. There are very good examples of all these ways of transferring heat energy in the living and human-made world.

Conduction

When you stir a hot liquid with a metal spoon, the spoon soon becomes hot. The metal has conducted the heat from the liquid into the spoon. This conduction is a result of vibrating molecules.

When molecules are heated, they vibrate and bump into one another. This allows the heat energy to be transferred from one molecule to another all the way along the metal spoon. A little heat energy is lost each time the energy is transferred, so not all the heat will be conducted. The amount of energy lost depends on the

This computer image shows the distribution of heat in a car that has just stopped. The white areas are the hottest. Some of the heat has been conducted by the metal parts of the car.

Would food cook more quickly in an oven dish made from glass or from metal?

substance involved. Metals are good conductors, since most of the heat energy is transferred. Saucepans are made of metal, so that the heat from the flame is quickly transferred to the food being cooked. But substances such as wool, cotton, plastic and air are all poor conductors of heat. This is because they contain a lot of air spaces. Air is a gas that conducts heat quite slowly. These materials are used as insulators to slow down the transfer of heat.

Convection

Why do you feel a draft when a fire burns strongly in a room or outside?

Radiators can quickly heat the air around them. Although air is a poor conductor of heat when it is trapped, moving air can carry heat energy around a room. As the molecules in the air gain heat energy from the radiator, they move around more rapidly, carrying the heat with them. The air expands as it warms up, so the same mass of air now occupies a larger volume. The density of a substance is calculated by dividing its mass by its volume, so as the volume increases, the density decreases. The warm air is now less dense than the colder air in the rest of the room, so it rises upward. As it does so, the cooler air is drawn toward the radiator to replace it. This creates a circulation of air called a convection current. The hot water supply in many houses works on a similar principle. The boiler heats the water, and as the warm water rises toward the storage tank, cold water is drawn into the bottom of the boiler ready to be heated. The hot water enters at the top of the storage tank and is released from the bottom when faucets are turned on.

A flock of pelicans spiraling upward on a thermal, high above the Rift Valley in Kenya.

Convection currents are very useful in the natural world. Many large birds, such as pelicans and vultures, use them to glide over great distances. Thermals are rising currents of warm air, often found over warm parts of the land. Birds circle within the column of rising air, gaining height, and then glide down before rising again on another thermal. The same principle is used in glider flying. By flying from thermal to thermal, unpowered gliders can often travel considerable distances. Winds, too, are created by convection currents, but on a global scale. The air at the equator is heated up more than air near the poles. This hot air rises and is replaced by cooler air from the regions to the north and south of the equator. This creates air movements which, in turn, produce winds.

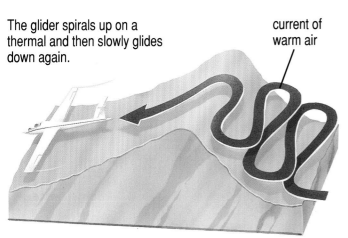

The glider spirals up on a thermal and then slowly glides down again.

current of warm air

Radiation

Ten people dancing in a room will give off more heat energy than a gas fire.

Hot objects give out invisible light and heat energy called infrared radiation. Like all forms of light, it travels in straight lines. The elements of a space heater radiate heat. Heat energy will be absorbed by the part of your body facing the heater. This will make you feel warm. The rest of your body will feel cold. Heating appliances are each designed to spread heat in different ways. A space heater spreads heat mainly by radiation. A radiator is designed to spread heat by convection (the warmed air creates currents in the room). But there is always some overlap between one system and another. In the radiator, for example, the metal conducts heat and if you put your hand very close to the pipe, you will feel radiated heat.

The heat energy from the sun cannot reach the earth by conduction or convection currents, because neither of these ways of transferring heat is possible in the vacuum of space. The earth is warmed up by radiation of heat energy from the sun.

The color of a surface affects how much heat energy is absorbed. Dark colored clothes absorb heat better than light-colored ones, so in winter we tend to wear darker colored clothing. In summer, paler clothes are more popular because the lighter surfaces reflect more of the heat. Shiny or highly polished surfaces absorb the least heat of all, because they reflect nearly all of the radiation that strikes them. The space shuttle has highly reflective

---

EXPERIMENT

Colored surfaces

In this experiment you will discover which color surfaces are better at absorbing heat energy. You will need four jam jars with lids, some black, red, and white paint, a paintbrush, some Plasticine (oil-based modeling clay), a hand drill, a long thermometer and some water.

1 Drill a hole in the center of each jar's lid. The hole should be just large enough to insert the thermometer.

2 Paint the outside of three of the jam jars, each a different color, leaving the fourth jar unpainted.

3 Fill each jar with cold water and screw the lids shut.

4 Use some Plasticine to block the hole in each lid, in order to stop any heat from escaping.

5 Place all the jars in a warm place, such as on a sunny window ledge or in front of a radiator or other heat source.

6 Every few minutes, remove the Plasticine briefly to take a temperature reading from each jar. Replace the Plasticine when you have taken the reading. Which jar warmed up most quickly? How could you make this experiment more accurate?

? *Why do marathon runners wrap themselves in Mylar "space blankets" after a race?*

Marathon runners in "space blankets" at the end of a race.

The space shuttle is equipped with black and white insulation tiles. The tiles will reflect heat away from the shuttle as it re-enters the earth's atmosphere.

tiles to reflect the heat as it passes through the earth's atmosphere.

An open fire or a simple space heater can only heat a small part of the room by radiation. Convection is a much better way of heating living spaces, which is why radiators or electric convection heaters are used in modern homes.

 Why are houses in hot countries often painted white?

Shape and size

The shape and size of an object are important when considering heat loss. If a large block of ice and a small block of ice are placed in the sun, the smaller block will melt more quickly than the large one. In the same way, if a small piece of rock is placed in the sun beside a large piece of rock, the smaller one will warm up more quickly. The reason for this has to do with the ratio of surface area to volume. The smaller pieces of ice and rock have a large surface area relative to their volume. This enables them to lose or gain heat more quickly. To absorb a lot of heat quickly, it is better to have a large surface area and a relatively small volume. But to retain heat longer, it is better to have a small surface area and a large volume. This important principle affects the shape and design of animals living in cold and warm regions of the world.

Key words
Conduction the transfer of heat by vibrating molecules.
Convection the movement of warm air currents.
Radiation the emission of heat from a hot object.

Keeping warm

Heat energy is essential to all forms of life. If the contents of a living cell freeze, the cell will rupture, just as the water in a frozen pipe expands to form crystals of ice. Animals living in the coldest parts of the world have to conserve their body heat in order to keep their cells from freezing. For humans to live and work in the Arctic and Antarctic, as well as in deep, cold water, they have to develop means of survival in very cold conditions. Some animals have evolved very effective ways of conserving heat. Scientists have studied these methods and incorporated them into energy-saving devices.

This diver is wearing a dry suit that has a layer of air between the skin and the suit to reduce heat loss. This enables the diver to stay in the water longer.

Surviving the cold

The mountain goat that lives in the Rockies survives nine months of winter with temperatures that fall to -50°C (-58°F). Its coat is long, shaggy and white, a color that is not good for absorbing heat (see page 10). Although white is useful camouflage in the snow, this is not the reason for its color, since there are no large

Mountain goats have a thick white coat that traps air to insulate against heat loss. Human mountaineers rely on clothing that also has a layer of air trapped within the fabric.

predators to threaten the goat. Why then should its coat be white? The answer concerns the structure of the hair that forms the coat. The hairs are hollow and transparent to ultraviolet light. Ultraviolet light is not visible to our eyes. The hairs conduct the ultraviolet light from the sun directly to the skin, where the light energy is transformed into heat energy. Heat loss is reduced by the goat's thick fur, which contains numerous air spaces to insulate the animal. Polar bears have identical hairs in their coat. In addition, the skin of the polar bear is black so that it can absorb as much heat energy as possible. This design is so efficient at retaining heat energy that, when viewed using infrared cameras that detect heat emissions, polar bears are found to give off no heat at all.

The Emperor penguin is the only animal that is able to survive the extreme cold of the Antarctic winter. Like many other animals, penguins huddle together to stay warm. No bird could survive the extreme cold on the outside of the huddle for very long, so the birds slowly move within the huddle, taking turns standing on the outside. A bird on the outside will slowly shuffle forward so that, after a while, it will be on the inside of the huddle.

Emperor penguins have long, fine feathers with tips that turn in toward the body. At the base of the feathers are fluffy tufts that stick together, forming an insulating layer. Unlike other birds, the penguin's feathers extend down its legs, providing additional insulation.

Seals have much thinner fur than penguins. The fur retains a thin layer of water, rather like a diver's rubber wet suit, so that the seal loses less heat. Seals also have an insulating layer of oily fat, called blubber, just beneath the skin.

Icefish living in the freezing waters of the North Atlantic

EXPERIMENT

Huddling

In this experiment you will prove that huddling reduces heat loss. You will need 10 small jam jars (or, better still, test tubes) some warm water and a long thermometer. If you are using test tubes, you will need to use something to keep them from falling over. You could hold them together in a bundle with string and use books to support them.

1 Position the jam jars or test tubes so that they are touching each other in a "huddle."

2 Fill the jam jars or test tubes to within 2 cm or a little less than an inch of the top of each with warm water.

3 Take the temperature of the water in all of the jars or test tubes.

4 Continue to take temperature readings of each jar in turn every five minutes for the next 20 minutes. Which jars or test tubes cool down more quickly?

have to make their own "antifreeze" to stop their body fluids from freezing. Cells in their bodies produce a special protein that sticks to ice crystals to stop them from growing. Scientists are studying genetic engineering techniques that would allow them to insert the gene for making this protein into bacteria. These altered bacteria could be grown in huge vats, to make large quantities of the protein for use on roads, on crops and on airplanes as a natural antifreeze. One day, the gene may even be inserted into plants, so that they can make their own antifreeze and survive frosts.

Some insects use their own "antifreeze" too. Their tissues contain a chemical called glycerol. Glycerol helps to protect cells from freezing by lowering the freezing point of water, thereby reducing the chances of ice crystals forming within the cells. Human-made antifreeze is used in the cooling systems of cars, so that the water does not freeze during cold weather. It works by lowering the freezing point of the water in the cooling system, just like the glycerol produced by insects. If the cooling water were allowed to freeze, it would expand and crack the car's radiator or cooling pipes.

Antifreeze prevents ice from forming in the car's radiator.

This icefish can live in extremely cold water because it has a natural antifreeze in its cells.

Insulation

The amount of heat energy lost from a house can be greatly reduced by placing a thick layer of insulation in the attic.

The Inuit people live in the Arctic and have adapted well to life in such an extreme climate. They often have short, stout bodies that are better suited to heat conservation than tall, thin ones. (See page 11 on surface area). But they would still not be able to survive if it were not for the insulation provided by the clothes they wear. Their traditional clothing is made from sealskin, polar bear skin and caribou pelts.

Today, there are artificial fibers that copy the heat-retaining action of fur and feathers in animals. Finely spun polyester is a soft and light insulator. The air spaces incorporated into the material increase its thermal efficiency (its ability to retain heat). Polyester is low in bulk and light in weight. Because it is soft and flexible, it can mold to the shape of the body and prevent air movements. The insulating air layer stays in place, trapping body heat.

Good insulation in a house will mean lower fuel bills and will

Can you think of any other ways to insulate your home, apart from attic insulation?

Mountain lizards in Peru can warm up their bodies from -2°C to over 30°C (28.4°F–86°F) in just one hour, even though the surface air temperature remains near the freezing point.

This collared lizard is basking on a rock to absorb heat energy from the sun.

help to conserve the supplies of fossil fuels. New houses now have an energy rating that indicates how good they are at retaining heat energy. It is even possible to check where heat losses are occurring in a building by using a video camera that can detect infrared radiation. By looking at the outside of a house through the camera, it is possible to tell where the heat loss originates.

Reptiles, fish, amphibians and all invertebrate animals are ectothermic, or cold-blooded. They have little insulation to help retain their body heat. Their body temperature is similar to that of their environment. If their bodies are cold, they do not work efficiently, so many ectothermic animals warm themselves up by lying in the sun and absorbing heat energy. Reptiles can often be seen basking on rocks in the early part of the day. The best habitats for ectothermic animals are those environments that are warm all year round. In parts of the world that are warm in summer and cold in winter, the ectotherms are only active during the warm months. They survive the coldest winter months by hibernating. To increase the amount of heat energy they absorb, many amphibians and reptiles can change their color by altering the size of the pigment cells in their skin. They can make these cells smaller or larger, thus decreasing or increasing the areas of dark pigment. Since dark colors absorb more heat than light ones, the animals can get warmer by making their skin darker (see page 10). They can also improve heat absorption by maximizing the surface area of their body facing the sun. They do this by spreading their legs, flattening their body and, in some cases, even raising special flaps of skin. The horned toad of North American deserts changes color during the day. In the morning its skin is dark to absorb heat so that it can become active quickly. But as the air temperatures start to rise, the color of its skin becomes lighter. This reflects heat and enables the toad to stay in the sun for much longer before it starts to overheat.

Insulation

In this experiment you will discover which materials provide the best insulation. You will need four small jam jars, a long thermometer, some Plasticine, some warm water and a selection of insulating materials, such as feathers, newspaper, aluminium foil and a roll of sterile cotton (available at pharmacies).

1 Make a hole large enough for your thermometer in each jam jar lid. Screw the lid in place.

2 Wrap a different type of insulation around three of the jars. Cover three lids too, but leave the holes clear. Leave one of the jam jars with no insulation at all.

3 Carefully fill all the jars three-quarters full of warm water. Secure the lids in place. Make a note of the temperature of the water in each jar. Cover the holes in the lids with Plasticine when the thermometer is not in use.

4 Take temperature readings from each jar every five minutes.

Which material provided the best insulation? How could you improve the design of this experiment? Did you use similar amounts of insulation? How could you make sure that this is a fair test?

You could repeat this experiment with just one type of insulation, but using jam jars of different sizes.

Heat exchangers

Whales have heat exchangers in their flippers so that the blood circulating through the flipper does not lose heat to the cold water.

Animals that live in cold climates cannot afford to lose too much of their body heat to the environment. All mammals and birds are endotherms, which means that they maintain a constant body temperature whatever the temperature of the surroundings.

Whales, living in water just a few degrees above freezing point (0°C or 32°F), cannot afford to lose much body heat. Whales have a thick layer of blubber for insulation around most of their body, but this would be impractical around their flippers, which must be able to move easily. Flippers have a relatively large surface area and are poorly insulated. The flippers need a good blood supply since they do a lot of work. However, a lot of heat could be lost as warm blood from the body circulates around the flipper. Excessive

Heat exchangers, natural and human-made

Whales have heat exchangers in their flippers (right) to make sure that valuable heat energy is not lost to the cold water. In a condensing boiler (far right) hot waste gases are cooled and the heat energy is transferred to water.

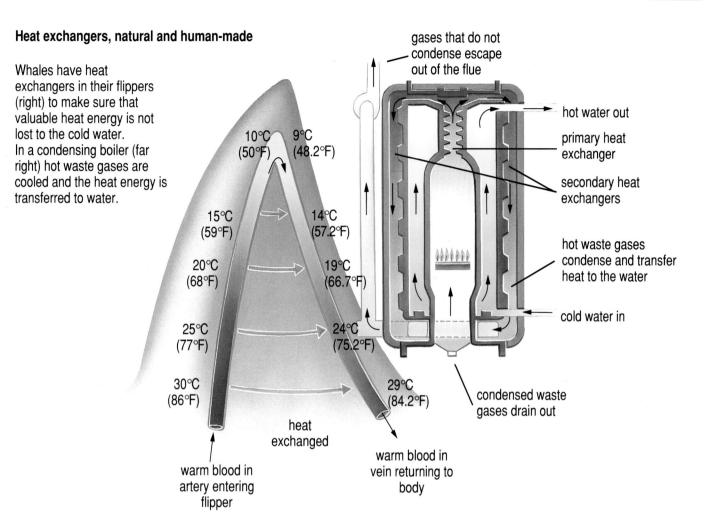

gases that do not condense escape out of the flue

hot water out

primary heat exchanger

secondary heat exchangers

hot waste gases condense and transfer heat to the water

cold water in

condensed waste gases drain out

10°C (50°F) 9°C (48.2°F)

15°C (59°F) 14°C (57.2°F)

20°C (68°F) 19°C (66.7°F)

25°C (77°F) 24°C (75.2°F)

30°C (86°F) 29°C (84.2°F)

heat exchanged

warm blood in artery entering flipper

warm blood in vein returning to body

Key words
Endotherm an animal whose body temperature stays constant regardless of changes in the environmental temperature.
Ectotherm an animal that relies on external heat sources to maintain its body temperature.
Insulation a layer of material that retains heat.

heat loss is prevented by the special way in which the blood vessels are arranged. In the whale, the artery that carries warm blood from the body into the flipper is completely surrounded by veins. So as warm arterial blood flows into the flipper, it is cooled by the cold venous blood returning to the body. By the time the arterial blood reaches the outside of the flipper, it is quite cool, and little heat is lost to the water. In contrast, the venous blood gains heat from the arterial blood, so by the time it returns to the core of the body, it is at body temperature. This type of system is known as a heat exchanger.

A boiler also works on the principle of heat exchange. Fuel is burned in a combustion chamber, and the heat given off is transferred to the water that flows in pipes through the boiler. However, burning fuel in this way produces a lot of hot waste gas that is vented to the outside of the building by a flue. These hot gases contain a lot of heat energy that is wasted. The newest boilers have been designed to extract as much of the heat from the waste gases as possible. These new models are called condensing boilers, since the heat exchanger also cools the waste gases with the cold water that enters the boiler. The drop in temperature causes the gases to condense and release almost all their heat energy to the water. This development has improved the energy efficiency of gas-fired boilers from 70 to 95 percent.

Keeping cool

Biological detergents do not work very well at high temperatures. Can you guess why?

There are many reasons why a living organism needs to keep cool. The most important is to keep chemicals called enzymes at their ideal temperature. Enzymes are catalysts (chemicals that begin a reaction or increase the rate at which it takes place). For example, when we eat food containing starch, enzymes in the mouth break the starch down into sugar. This reaction only takes a few seconds in the presence of the enzyme, but without it the reaction could take hours, if not days. However, enzymes need to be at a particular temperature to work in the most effective way. If the body temperature becomes too hot, the enzymes are damaged and stop working. If the body becomes too cold, the enzymes also stop working, but they are inactivated rather than damaged.

Evaporation

Dogs cannot sweat, so they have to pant to keep cool.

Crocodiles keep cool by opening their mouths wide, so that water can evaporate from a large surface.

It takes at least 2,500,000 J of heat energy to change 1 kilogram of water into vapor.

Similar methods for keeping cool are used by living organisms, in human-made buildings and in machines. Heat can be lost in four ways: by conduction, convection, radiation and evaporation. The first three methods were discussed on pages 8, 9 and 10. The fourth, evaporation, occurs when a liquid is changed into a gas. The liquid is said to have changed state. An example of a change of state occurs when water boils. Water boils at 100 °C (212°F) and a lot of steam is seen rising from the surface of the water. The water has changed state from a liquid into a gas—water vapor. However, water does not have to be boiling for evaporation to occur. Water will also evaporate from clothes hanging outside to dry. The water evaporates because some of the water molecules are moving faster than others. Fast-moving molecules near the surface of the water may escape and form a gas.

A lot of heat energy is needed to make the water molecules move faster so that some evaporate. This heat energy is taken from the water. Evaporation therefore cools down the water. For example, it takes just 418 J to heat 1 g (.035oz.) of water from 0 °C to 100 °C (32°F to 212°F), but it takes six times as much heat

African elephants have large ears that they flap to keep themselves cool.

If you place perfume or rubbing alcohol on your skin, it quickly disappears and your skin feels cold. Why?

A person in a desert could lose 1.5 liters (1.59 qt.) of sweat per hour through evaporation. If the person had no water to drink he or she could die from dehydration within 12 hours.

energy to change 1 g of water into water vapor.

Many animals use evaporation to help to control their body temperature. Some mammals, such as humans, sweat to keep cool. Sweat is a liquid that contains water, salts and urea (a waste product produced by the liver). The heat energy needed to evaporate the sweat is taken from the skin, so the skin is cooled. Cattle, camels, humans and horses can sweat, but other mammals, such as dogs, cannot. They keep cool by panting or licking themselves. Panting increases the amount of evaporation that can take place from the mouth. Cats often lick themselves to spread saliva over their fur. The saliva evaporates and cools the cat's body. Crocodiles, like many reptiles, keep cool by using a technique called thermal gaping; they open their mouths wide to expose a large surface area over which water can evaporate.

Another way of keeping cool is to circulate blood close to the surface of the skin so that more of the blood's heat can reach the surface. You may have noticed that, when people become hot, they become red in the face. This is because more blood is passing through the blood vessels close to the surface of the skin. This moves warmth to the outside of the body where it can be lost quickly by evaporation.

Animals that live in warm tropical climates tend to have a large surface area over which heat can be lost. Typically, they have large ears and long thin limbs. The bat-eared fox, for example, loses much of its excess body heat through the blood vessels in its oversized ears. Elephants, too, lose heat from their ears, but they also use them as fans to circulate air over the surface of the skin. By comparison, animals living in the colder parts of the world tend to have short ears and stocky limbs in order to reduce their overall ratio of mass to surface area.

Temperature control is very important in a beehive. In summer, the average temperature of a beehive is about 35 °C (95°F), and it varies very little. This temperature is ideal for the

If a beehive gets too hot, the worker bees fan their wings to bring in fresh, cooler air from outside.

growth of the young bee larvae that develop rapidly while there is plenty of food to be found. If the temperature rises, the worker bees spread water droplets over the comb. These droplets evaporate and so cool down the hive. Groups of worker bees can also increase the cooling effect by fanning their wings to create air currents. The drafts bring in cooler dry air and help to get rid of the saturated warm air, thereby aiding the evaporation process. If the outside temperature falls, the worker bees huddle together. The warmest place is in the middle of the cluster, so the bees all try to work their way toward the center. By clustering in this way, the bees help each other to survive low temperatures that would kill an individual bee (see page 13).

Refrigerators

Why does frost form on windows on cold nights?

Refrigerators are used to keep food cool and so help it stay fresh longer. They work using a process that also involves evaporation. A liquid refrigerant that will evaporate easily is circulated around the refrigerator. When the refrigerant evaporates, it takes up heat energy. When it condenses back into a liquid state, it releases the heat energy again. The refrigerant is contained within a long, coiled tube that runs between the inside of the refrigerator and the outside. During its path through the refrigerator, the refrigerant is changed from liquid to vapor and then back into liquid form. When the refrigerant enters the evaporator coils, near the center of the refrigerator, it is evaporated, forming a vapor within the coils. As it changes state it absorbs heat energy from the air inside, creating a cooling effect in the refrigerator. As the vaporized refrigerant passes along the radiator grill at the back of the refrigerator, it is compressed by a pump. This raises the temperature of the refrigerant above room temperature, causing it to condense. Heat energy is given off into the air as the refrigerant condenses and passes once more into the evaporator coils.

This refrigerator is cooled by a refrigerant that can be used over and over again.

Modern air conditioners work on a similar principle. A complete system not only controls the temperature of the air but also its humidity. An air conditioner can also remove dust and odors. To do this, the air is moved by a fan through a refrigeration unit, before being filtered and passed over charcoal for odor removal.

Transpiration

Evaporation of water also takes place from the surface of plant leaves. This process is called transpiration. The main role of transpiration is not to keep the plant cool but to ensure the movement of water and minerals from the roots to the shoots. This is rather like drinking from a straw; suction at the top draws the liquid upward. In the same way, evaporating water from the top of the plant creates a suction that will draw water up from the roots. Even though the cooling effect of transpiration is not very important for the plant, it has many benefits to people. When you walk under trees on a hot summer's day, it is noticeable how much cooler it is under the trees than in the open. The air has been cooled by transpiration. City planners are now making much greater use of trees as natural air conditioners. Trees have, in fact, been used in this way for many hundreds of years. For example, the Moors, who ruled southern Spain from 711 to 1492, liked to use trees in their courtyards for their cooling effects. At the Expo '92 site in Seville, Spain, where temperatures can get very high in summer, all the walkways were lined with trees and the sitting areas were in the shade of trees. There were human-made cooling mechanisms as well. Special cooling towers used atomizers to cool the air. Atomizers were used to spray millions of tiny droplets of water into the air. The droplets evaporated in the heat, cooling the surrounding air, and as the warm water vapor rose, convection currents drew in more air at the bottom, creating refreshing breezes.

The trees in this park in Hong Kong cool the surrounding air as they transpire. Huge atomizers at Expo '92 in Spain (top right) sprayed millions of water droplets into the air, which evaporated and cooled the air.

Key words
Evaporation the process in which water changes from its liquid state to a vapor, using heat energy.
Transpiration the evaporation of water from the leaves of a plant.

Energy from the sun

Almost all the fuel on earth originates from just one place – the sun. The sun is a remarkable source of free light and heat energy, often referred to as solar energy. This energy is produced in a massive nuclear chain reaction that takes place inside the sun. This reaction continuously releases huge quantities of energy in all directions. Much of the light and heat energy that reaches the earth is reflected straight back into space by the atmosphere or is absorbed by the atmosphere itself. Only a tiny fraction of the sun's energy ever reaches the surface of the planet, but this is enough to support life as we know it. The amount of usable solar energy varies considerably over the earth's surface, with some areas receiving much more than others.

Solar cells (above) and leaves (right) both use energy from the sun.

Plants and light energy

The leaves of these rainforest trees are spread out toward the sun to trap the maximum amount of light energy.

Of all living organisms, it is the green plants that make the greatest use of light energy from the sun. Green plants have evolved the ability to trap the light energy in sunlight, concentrate it and convert it into "fuel" that can be stored within plant cells. As far as the plants are concerned, this energy is free and readily available. The energy that plants convert into chemical energy forms the basis of all food chains. Almost all animals, including humans, are dependent upon plants for life because animals are unable to transform light energy directly into chemical energy. They rely on plants to supply this energy, either directly (by eating the plants themselves) or indirectly (by eating other animals that eat plants).

Plants developed the ability to use light energy millions of years ago. They trap light energy using large, flat solar panels called leaves. This light energy is changed into chemical energy in a process called photosynthesis. Then this chemical energy can either be used in respiration in the cells (see page 42) or stored for future use. As yet, humans have been unable to capture light energy in such an effective way.

In less than one hour, the earth receives energy from the sun that is equivalent to the total energy released from all other sources in an entire year.

Parasitic plants do not contain any chlorophyll. How do they obtain their food?

The process of photosynthesis is quite a complex one, but the following simple equation summarizes the process:

light + carbon dioxide + water = food (glucose) + oxygen

First, the light energy has to be trapped. The cells in plant leaves contain a green pigment called chlorophyll that allows plants to use light energy. When light falls on a molecule of chlorophyll, it absorbs the light energy and becomes excited. This results in a series of reactions that end in the production of glucose (a simple sugar) and oxygen. The glucose may be used as an energy source for respiration and new growth, or it may be converted into starch for storage. Sometimes the starch is stored in special parts of the plant, such as the roots or the seeds. The other product of photosynthesis, oxygen, passes out of the leaf into the air. The oxygen is a very important by-product, since it is required by most living organisms for respiration. Respiration is a chemical process in the cell that releases energy from foods such as glucose. Respiration uses oxygen and produces carbon dioxide. Plants respire too, so some of the oxygen they produce in photosynthesis is used for respiration in their own cells.

Solar collectors and cells

The solar cells that power this telecom relay station in Northern Australia point toward the sun to capture the maximum amount of light energy.

Both the heat and light energy from the sun can be captured and transformed into other forms of energy by using solar collectors and cells. Solar energy is particularly useful in remote areas where it is not practical to distribute power by electric transmission lines. It is also useful in developing countries where the supply of electricity is intermittent. More than 6,000 villages in India use solar energy.

Solar collectors have a large, flat surface designed to trap the heat energy from the sun and use it to heat water or air. The simplest design is a black plate that will absorb heat energy when placed in sunlight. Water is pumped over the black plate and, as the water flows across the plate, the heat energy from the plate is absorbed. An even simpler design is a glass wall that allows the air behind the glass to be heated directly. These walls are positioned on the south side of a building. The glass allows the light and heat energy into the building. Just as in a greenhouse, the reflected light energy is trapped and warms the

Solar power is not a new discovery—3,000 years ago a palace in Turkey was warmed using water heated by the sun!

air inside the building. At night a black curtain is put across the glass wall to keep the heat energy from escaping into the cooler air outside.

In northern Europe, where there are many overcast days, solar collectors are a less reliable means of meeting energy needs than in sunny countries. A good alternative design is the heat store. This consists of a large hole in the ground, lined with black plastic, containing a large amount of water. During the day, the black lining absorbs heat energy from the sun and transfers it to the bottom layer of water. The water can be pumped out to provide heat at night. Then it is returned for reheating again and again. This system is best suited to provide heat at night. If the heat store is dug deep and large enough, the heat can be stored for weeks.

Solar or photovoltaic cells change light energy directly into electric energy. Solar cells are made from wafers of semiconductor, material that can conduct electricity under certain circumstances. This material can transform light directly into electricity. There are two separate layers of semiconductors within a cell. When light energy hits the cell, electric charges move between the two layers and this produces a current of electricity. More light shining on the cell produces more electricity.

Unfortunately, there is still no efficient way of storing and recovering the electric energy that is produced using solar energy. Most electric energy from solar cells is wasted if it is not used up as soon as it is converted. However, a trial is being conducted in New England in which houses fitted with solar cells have special connections to the main electric power grid. If the solar cells do not make enough electricity, then the houses draw electricity from the grid. When the solar cells produce a surplus of energy, they feed the surplus into the grid and the electric meters go backward! This development means that on sunny days the output of electricity from the main fossil fuel power stations can be reduced.

The wall behind the windows of this house in Wales is painted black to absorb heat energy, helping to warm up the air in the house.

In summer these solar panels absorb heat energy, which is used to heat an underground store of water. The water retains the heat energy, which can be used in winter to heat homes.

Solar power stations

The parabolic reflector of this solar furnace in Odeilo, France, is composed of 9,500 mirrors. The mirrors reflect sunlight onto the furnace (central tower) in front of the reflector.

!

If solar collectors covered only 0.1 percent of the Mojave Desert in California, they could supply Los Angeles with all its electricity.

Key words
Photosynthesis the process of making sugar and starch using light energy in green plants.
Solar cell a device that directly converts light energy into electricity.
Solar collector a device that uses heat energy from the sun to heat water.

The first solar power stations consisted of thousands of solar collectors covering a large area. The collectors were connected to a central heat exchanger that produced steam. The steam in turn powered an electric generator. However, a lot of heat energy was lost as it was transferred to the central heat exchanger. Some more recent designs involve an array of mirrors around a central power collection tower. The sun's rays are focused at the top of the tower by the mirrors and the heat energy is collected by black pipes that contain liquid sodium (a substance with a much higher boiling point than water). Heat exchangers in the tower are connected to boilers (see page 17) that produce steam to drive turbines.

A further refinement is the construction of a "solar furnace," so that the liquid is raised to very high temperatures, making the power station even more efficient. One of the best known solar furnaces is in Odeilo, France. On a hillside, 11,000 flat mirrors follow the sun and reflect its rays onto a huge wall of curved mirrors covering the side of a 10-story building. The curved mirrors refocus the sun's rays onto an area less than one meter square where the temperature reaches 3,300°C (5,972°F).

Transforming energy

Animals have to be able to unlock the energy found in food and transform it into a form of energy that their bodies can use.

Much of the energy that is available to people is in a form that cannot be used. The energy has to be converted into a form that we can use.

A common form of energy that people use is electric energy or electricity. Electricity is a particularly important and useful form of energy to both people and animals. Some animals can generate their own electricity using special organs within their bodies. Human-made electricity can be generated in several different ways, for example, using fuels or light energy as well as the energy from wind and waves.

Electricity

When you dry your hair with a hairdryer, 20 trillion electrons pass along the wire every second.

Electricity is a type of energy that has many different uses. But what exactly is electricity? In order to understand the nature of electricity it is important to examine the structure of the atom.

All matter consists of tiny particles called atoms, and each atom is itself composed of three smaller types of particle. In the center of the atom is a heavy nucleus containing protons and neutrons. The nucleus is surrounded by a cloud of much smaller moving particles called electrons. The protons have a positive charge while the electrons have a negative charge. These charges cancel each other out so that the atom is neutral. This means that the atom has neither a positive nor a negative charge.

Electrons are very small and are easy to move. For example, simply rubbing a cloth along a plastic rod will cause some electrons to be transferred from the rod to the cloth. The rod will become positively charged. This is because its atoms have lost electrons and now contain more positive charges than negative charges. The cloth will gain electrons. So the atoms in the cloth will have more negatively charged electrons than positive protons, giving it an overall negative charge.

Objects that have opposite charges attract each other. In the example above, the positively charged rod will attract the negatively charged cloth. This is often felt as static electricity.

Any substance can become electrically charged, but only conductors allow a current to flow. The best conductors are metals, such as copper and gold, although many other materials also conduct electricity to some degree. The word *current* does not really describe how electrons move along a wire, for in fact each electron does not move very far at all. Instead, individual electrons bump into each other in turn, passing on energy. A current of electric energy is produced. This current of electric

Static electricity has caused the hairs on this wig to stand up.

energy is measured in amperes (A). The current is measured using an instrument called an ammeter.

Any material that does not allow current to flow is known as an insulator. For example, the plastic sleeve around a piece of electric cable (which is usually copper) is an insulator. The insulator is used to make sure that the electric current does not flow to a place where it is not wanted or where it could cause injury or damage.

EXPERIMENT

Conductors and insulators

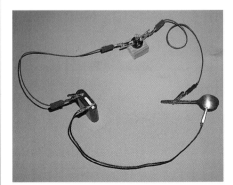

In this simple experiment you will discover which household items are conductors and which are insulators. You will need a battery, such as those used in a radio or flashlight, three electric leads (insulated wires), a small bulb and a selection of kitchen items made from different materials. For example, you can use scissors, plastic spoons, metal spoons, cookie sheets, foil, plates, matches and string.

1 First connect the three wires, battery and bulb to make a circuit. Check that the bulb lights up. Then insert one test item into the circuit as shown in the photograph.

2 If the material of the test item conducts electricity, the light bulb will light up. If the material is an insulator, the bulb will stay unlit. Try each item in turn and record your results.

Electromagnetism

In power stations, much of the chemical energy from the fuel is lost as heat energy. The cooling towers cause the hot steam to condense back into water.

Most of the electricity that is used in the home and in industry is generated or produced using a dynamo. This involves the transformation of kinetic energy into electric energy. In 1831, Michael Faraday became the first scientist to discover that electricity was produced when a wire was moved between the poles of a magnet. The kinetic energy of the moving wire had been transformed into electric energy. The amount of electricity produced can be increased by coiling the wire and spinning it very quickly in a magnetic field. The larger the coil and the faster it spins, the more electricity is produced.

Power stations use extremely large dynamos to generate electricity. Their source of energy is variable, but it is usually a fossil fuel such as coal, gas or oil. The fuel contains stored energy that is released when the fuel is burned in oxygen. This releases lots of heat energy, which is then used to heat water to make steam. The steam is under very high pressure, and this produces a very large force that can turn huge steam turbines. The spinning turbines are attached to large electromagnetic coils. As the coils spin they produce a current that can then be used by consumers.

Alternative energy sources

People have known for a very long time that moving water is a source of kinetic energy that can be very useful. In the past, running water was used in mills to turn large water wheels that

Water stored behind the dam in the reservoir is used to spin a turbine (inset) inside the dam. When the turbine spins, kinetic energy is transformed into electric energy.

What energy transformations are involved in producing electricity using turbines in dams?

would then turn a millstone. The millstone could grind grain into flour. Today, fast-flowing water is used to generate hydroelectricity. A lot of hydroelectricity is produced near dams built across rivers. The dams create reservoirs to store the water for when it is needed. The water behind the dam has potential energy. As a controlled amount of water from the reservoir is allowed to fall through pipes, it gains kinetic energy. Potential energy has been transformed into kinetic energy. The falling water is used to spin a turbine that, in turn, drives a generator to make electric energy. Sometimes the water is pumped back uphill using surplus power at times when there is little demand for electricity. The water can be released again during times of peak demand. In countries where there are many fast-flowing rivers that can be dammed, very large quantities of hydroelectricity can be generated. The mountainous countries of Norway and Sweden, for example, generate most of their electricity in this way. Small-scale dams can also be built on smaller rivers, where a drop in river height of just a few feet or so is sufficient to generate enough electricity to power a farm or even a small village. However, the building of even small dams can create environmental problems, because a dam floods large areas of land and affects the natural flow of water in the river.

Windmills have been built in windy places for thousands of years. They were originally used to turn millstones or pump water. More recently, technology has enabled wind energy to be harnessed to generate electricity. Modern wind generators are sometimes quite small and are grouped together to form wind farms. The conversion of wind energy is a relatively efficient form of energy conversion, for wind energy is converted first to kinetic energy and then directly to electrical energy, avoiding heat transformation and subsequent heat losses. Water and wind power are also renewable forms of energy. Unlike fossil fuels, they will not run out (see also pages 22–25 on solar power).

Wind farms, such as this one in California, are located in mountain passes and on hillsides where there is lots of wind all year round.

EXPERIMENT

Making electricity

You do not need a battery to produce an electric current. All that is needed is wire and a magnet. You will carry out a simple test to prove that an electric current can be produced by just moving a magnet into a coil of wire. This test is very similar to the experiment that Faraday carried out. You will need a length of wire, alligator clips, a bar magnet, a thick pencil or piece of wooden dowel and an

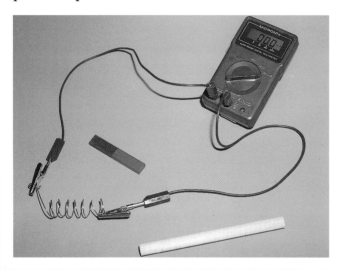

ammeter for measuring current. Modern multimeters can be set to measure current too.

1 Wrap the wire around the pencil or dowel to make a coil of wire of about 10 turns. Make sure the magnet can fit into the coil. If not, choose a thicker piece of wood or use several pencils together to make the coil wider.

2 Clip or wrap the ends of the wire to the ammeter.

3 Move the magnet in and out of the coil at different speeds. Watch the ammeter carefully as you do so. What happens to the reading on the ammeter if you move the magnet slowly? What happens when you move the magnet quickly?

4 Repeat the experiment, but this time make a coil with more turns of wire. What happens now?

Explanation When the magnet is moved into the coil, the electrons in the coil are moved by the magnetic field. This causes the current to flow around the circuit.

Animals and electricity

The strongest electric shocks in the living world are produced by the South American electric eel. It can deliver discharges of 500-600 V—easily powerful enough to kill other fish and even human beings.

Some sharks are so sensitive to electric discharges from muscle that they can find flat fish, at rest on the sea bed under a layer of sand, just from the movement of their gills.

Some fish, such as the electric eel, have developed the remarkable ability to generate very strong electric shocks. Although these shocks were first noticed by the ancient Greeks, their cause was not understood until the nature of electricity began to be discovered. Those fish that produce electric shocks do so as a protective measure to scare away predators. Even very weak electric discharges can be useful, since these give the fish important information about their environment. Such discharges can enable the animal to distinguish between non-conducting objects and conducting objects such as another animal. Electric discharges can also help a fish to navigate in murky water.

Most electric fish contain a special electric organ consisting of modified (altered) muscle. The electric eel has two very large electric organs, one running down each side of its body, which make up 40 percent of its body volume. These organs contain thin, waferlike cells called electroplates, which are stacked in columns. Each column may contain 10,000 such plates. The plates do not contract when they receive an impulse from the nervous system; instead, they send out electric pulses. They can generate shocks in excess of 300 V. The electric catfish, found in the Nile and Congo rivers, can generate electric shocks of a similar strength. However, fresh water does not conduct electricity as well as salt water, so the electric shocks produced by fish living in fresh water have a more limited range.

Other fish, while unable to produce electric discharges themselves, can detect weak electric activity from the muscle action of other animals, using special electroreceptors. Sharks and rays are able to locate prey, including humans, in this way. Electroreceptors are special sense organs in the skin, mostly in the head region. They are common among sharks and a number of bony fish. The electric eel not only produces a sizeable electric discharge but also has a sophisticated array of electroreceptors. These receptors produce a stream of 300 bursts of electrical energy per second. This creates an electric current flowing through the surrounding water. The extent of the electric current in the water is called an electrical field. Any object that enters this field will distort the shape of the field. The receptors are sensitive to such changes and can immediately detect the intruder.

Many fish, such as this elephant trunk fish from West Africa, have electric organs.

The duck-billed platypus uses electroreceptors in its bill to find shrimp on the riverbed.

Electric fish can learn a lot about other electric fish by studying their electric fields. They can discover the age, sex and emotional state of other fish.

Energy efficiency

In any energy conversion, some of the energy is converted into a form that is not required and may be considered as wasted energy. This is most often heat energy. The more energy that is converted into the form of energy that is required, the more efficient the energy conversion. Very few energy conversions are 100 percent efficient. One conversion that is almost 100 percent efficient is the conversion of electric energy to heat energy in a space heater. Some batteries are almost 90 percent efficient, but gasoline engines are only 25 percent efficient. That means that for every gallon of gas burned by the engine, only 25 percent of the chemical energy stored in the gas is changed into kinetic energy. Even animals are not much more efficient in converting energy. In respiration, only 40 percent of the chemical energy in glucose is changed into useful forms of energy. The rest is converted into heat energy. Some of this heat has a use, since it keeps our body temperature at 37 °C (98.6°F).

One important energy conversion in the natural world is the conversion of food into new body tissue. This, perhaps surprisingly, is not particularly efficient. When a cow eats grass, only 10–20 percent of the total energy locked up in the cells of the plant is taken up and built into the cells of the cow. The remaining 80–90 percent is wasted. For example, a cow will only eat the fresh green leaves of the grass. It will not eat the roots or old leaves, so these parts of the plant are wasted. When a cow eats grass, its digestive system cannot break down all of the plant cell walls, which are quite tough, so much of what the cow eats is passed out from the gut. The droppings of a cow contain a lot of energy locked up in the undigested grass. As a result, only a tiny fraction of the energy stored in a plant is used to make new cells in the cow. The same is true when people eat cows. We only eat the muscle and some of the organs, such as the liver. The rest of the cow, especially the skeleton, is not

A filament light bulb is very inefficient because only 3 percent of the electric energy is converted to light energy. A cow is more efficient since 10–20 percent of the energy locked up in grass is used to make new animal tissue.

This diagram shows what happens to the chemical energy locked up in food. Only a very small amount of the energy released by respiration will be used to do work.

heat energy

chemical energy in body wastes

growth and repair

work (e.g., moving muscles)

chemical energy in food

Energy losses in a food chain

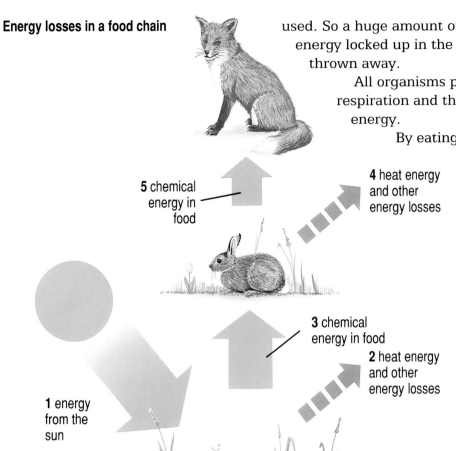

5 chemical energy in food

4 heat energy and other energy losses

3 chemical energy in food

2 heat energy and other energy losses

1 energy from the sun

used. So a huge amount of the cow is never eaten and the energy locked up in the wasted parts of the cow is thrown away.

All organisms produce heat energy as a result of respiration and this too represents a waste of energy.

By eating meat, a lot of energy is wasted in the food chain. In fact, the lower down the food chain we can eat, the more efficient the energy conversion will be. In a world where there is insufficient food to feed all the people, it would therefore be far more efficient for all of us to become vegetarians.

 Most food chains never have more than three or four energy transfers. Why are food chains with more transfers rare?

Each year, in a typical industrialized country, power stations release enough heat energy as waste to keep every home in the country warm!

In many developing countries, very little meat is eaten. The diet is mostly vegetarian with lots of rice or corn, together with vegetables and fruit.

Key words
Atom the smallest unit of a chemical that is still that chemical. It contains a nucleus and outer cloud of electrons.
Conductor a substance that allows electric currents to flow through it.
Electron a small negatively charged particle found in a cloud around the nucleus of an atom.
Insulator a substance that does not allow electric currents to flow through it.

Storing energy

Dry batteries store chemical energy that is transformed into electric energy to power electric goods such as toys, Walkmen and radios.

It is often very useful to be able to store energy for future use. The form in which energy is stored needs to be one that can be quickly converted into a form that can be used. Energy can be stored in many ways both by living organisms and by human-made objects. Many animals store energy in special cells in the form of fat. Plants store energy in the form of starch, which can be quickly broken down into glucose and respired (see pages 23 and 42). To supply our modern energy needs, we need a stored chemical energy of either fossil fuels or batteries. For example, every day we rely on stored energy in batteries to produce the electric current to work a piece of equipment such as a radio or a flashlight, or the stored energy in fuel to move a car.

Fossil fuels

These charcoal briquettes are made from slowly burning wood. They also contain stored chemical energy that can be transformed into heat energy.

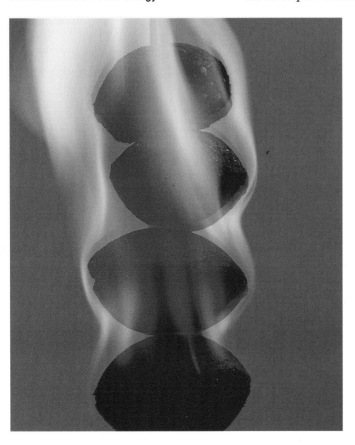

Fossil fuels is the name of a group of fuels that includes oil, gas, coal and peat. They are called fossil fuels because they have been made from the fossilized remains of living organisms that lived millions of years ago. For example, when marine animals such as primitive invertebrates died, they sank to the sea bed where they decayed and became covered with mud. Over a very long time a thick layer of mud and then rock formed over the dead bodies. The pressure from the layers of rock above crushed the dead organic matter into a liquid. Millions of years later, this liquid formed oil and gas.

Coal is made from ancient plant matter that has been slowly pressed under the great weight of overlying rock. There are several stages in the production of high-quality black coal. The first stage is the formation of peat from dead and decaying plant matter. The peat slowly gets buried by fresh layers of dead plant material. This compresses the peat. After further compression, the peat changes into brown coal or lignite. This type of coal only contains 70 percent carbon and is not as good as older coal. After a very long time and further compression, lignite will develop into a darker coal called anthracite that contains 90 percent carbon.

All these fossil fuels contain stored energy that was once part of living organisms. When the plants and animals died, the chemical energy locked up in their dead cells was stored. This stored energy is released when the fuel is burned, or oxidized, in the presence of oxygen.

Battery power

A simple dry cell battery

central electrode of carbon

zinc casing forms the second electrode

gel of ammonium chloride

Electric energy can be stored directly in devices called capacitors, but these devices can only store small amounts of electrical energy and they are quite bulky. Batteries, on the other hand, store chemical energy. When the battery is used, its stored chemical energy undergoes a reaction that creates electric energy.

There are many different types of batteries, but they all work on the same principle. Each battery, or cell, consists of two electrodes (usually pieces of metal) with a liquid or gel solution between them. When the battery is connected to an electric circuit, a chemical reaction takes place in the solution and this causes electrons to move toward one of the electrodes. This causes that electrode to become negatively charged, while the other electrode loses some electrons and becomes positively charged. If you study the outside of a dry battery, you will notice that one end is marked with a positive sign, and the other with a negative sign. A battery can be thought of as an electron pump. When the battery is connected to a circuit, it will pump out electrons from the negative terminal, creating a current. The electrons carry energy with them. As they flow around the circuit toward the positive terminal of the battery, they lose energy. For example the batteries in a Walkman pump out electric energy, which is transformed into kinetic energy. By the time the electrons return to the battery, they will have used up all of their energy. The amount of energy the electrons carry is measured in volts (V). Batteries with a higher voltage give their electrons more energy, so they can do more work than batteries of a lower voltage.

A battery will continue to produce an electric current until the chemicals are exhausted. Once the chemicals have been used up, the battery is dead and cannot provide any more energy to create electricity. It usually has to be thrown away. However, there are some dry batteries available that can be recharged by passing a small electric current through the battery for a number of hours. They are often referred to as nicads, because they have nickel and cadmium electrodes.

By joining a number of batteries, a larger electric force, or voltage, can be produced. Cars use large 12 V batteries made up of six cells in a series. Each cell has lead electrodes and contains an acid solution. The battery is known as a lead-acid battery. When the battery has become dead it can be recharged a limited number of times.

These lead-acid batteries are dead and cannot take any more charge. They contain acids that can be dangerous if the batteries are not disposed of carefully.

! *A nicad battery can be recharged up to 700 times.*

EXPERIMENT

A natural battery

Believe it or not, it is possible to make a battery using a lemon! All that is needed are two different pieces of metal and an acid solution. Since the juice in a lemon is slightly acidic, it can be made into a battery. You will

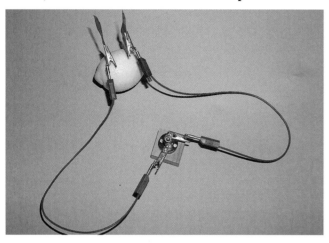

need a lemon, some copper wire, a 1.5V light bulb and holder, a strip of zinc and a strip of thin copper. You should be able to buy strips of these metals from a hardware store.

1 Cut two parallel slits in the top of the lemon, about 2 cm (.8 in) apart. Push a strip of zinc into one slit and a strip of copper into the other.

2 Now connect the zinc strip on the lemon to one terminal on the light bulb holder and the copper strip to the other terminal. You should now have a complete circuit and the bulb should glow.

Unfortunately your lemon battery will not last as long as a real battery, but it is much more fun! Where does the chemical energy in the lemon come from?

Biomass

 Compost heaps are very warm inside. Where does this heat come from?

Wood can be grown specifically for fuel, and so it is a type of renewable fuel. Once the trees have been harvested for wood, new trees can be planted. Plant material that can be used in this way is called biomass. Most plant material, including twigs, leaves, straw

 Why would planting more trees for biomass help to reduce the greenhouse effect?

The coppiced wood, a cluster of trees planted to be harvested on a rotation basis without killing the tree, is an example of a natural supply of chemical energy that renews itself.

It is estimated that, in the United States, the energy that could be generated from burning biomass such as garden waste, wood and waste paper would be equivalent to the output of 200 large nuclear power plants.

and even unwanted food can be used to generate energy. The plant matter can be dried and burned to provide energy for cooking and heating. Or it can be allowed to rot. When plant material rots, it releases a gas called methane that can be collected and burned to release energy.

Many countries are now planting fast-growing tree species that can be quickly harvested and used for fuel. In Ireland and Sweden, for example, willow and birch trees are grown for this purpose. Other species of tree used elsewhere include the cottonwood and poplar. These trees are not killed when they are harvested, but are cut off at ground level. New shoots soon appear from the cut stump, ready for harvest 10 to 15 years later. This type of treatment is called coppicing.

Natural storage

This onion has just started to grow. The new green leaves will use the chemical energy stored in the fleshy white leaf bases that make up most of the onion bulb.

Animals and plants also store energy for future use. Plants store chemical energy in the form of starch in their roots or in special organs such as tubers and bulbs. This energy store enables the plant to survive the winter and start to grow early in spring.

Plants also lay down stores of starch in their seeds, so the young plant will have a source of energy and be able to grow new roots and shoots. Starch is a very important food source for many animals, including humans, because of the amount of chemical energy it contains. Animals have energy stores too. When an animal consumes more energy than it needs, the excess energy is converted to fat. This fat is stored under the skin and around important organs. Mammals that hibernate eat large

Legumes are the seeds of the pea family —peas, beans and lentils. They are an important source of starch and protein in the human diet.

The dormouse is a small mammal that has to hibernate during the winter.

quantities of food in the summer and fall in order to build up their winter fat reserves. During hibernation, their heart rate slows down and they burn up the energy very slowly.

Most mammals shiver when they get cold in order to generate heat. But newborn mammals, including human babies, cannot shiver for some time after they are born. Nor can animals shiver while they are deep in hibernation.

 The body temperature of a hibernating mammal may fall as low as 3°C (37.4°F).

 How many different kinds of food can you think of that contain starch?

EXPERIMENT

Testing for starch

Starch is stored in several different places in a plant and is therefore found in a wide variety of foods. In this experiment, you will discover which types of food contain starch. You can also test seeds, flowers and bulbs for starch. You will require some iodine (this can be obtained from a drugstore), a selection of foods such as flour, cookies, bread, carrots, potato, onion, cheese and some petals from a white flower. You will also need a mortar and pestle (or small bowl and old wooden spoon), a knife and a test tube or a small see-through container.

1 Choose one food sample. Chop it into small pieces with the knife and grind it up in the mortar and pestle with a small amount of water.

2 Let the food and water mix settle for a few minutes and then pour off the water into the test tube or container.

3 Add a few drops of iodine to the water sample. If starch is present, the water will immediately become blue-black. If there is no starch, the water will turn the color of iodine (yellow).

Repeat the experiment using each of your food samples in turn. Did any of the results surprise you?

Note: Do not eat the foods after adding iodine.

The average adult expends between 8,000–12,000 kJ of energy per day. This is about the same as the heat output of a 100 W light bulb.

Instead, both rely on another form of heat production. They use the energy stored in brown fat. This type of tissue looks very different from that containing the usual fat. Brown fat is very valuable because a very small amount of brown fat can release huge amounts of energy. For example, a rat that weighs 300 g (10.5 oz.) may only have 1–2 g (.035–.07 oz.) of brown fat, but this can increase the total amount of heat released by the animal by nearly 100 percent. Scientists believe that the rapid rewarming of a hibernating mammal as it awakes is also helped by the energy stored in brown fat.

Deep heat stores

Geothermal energy sources provide energy for 3 million homes in the United States and heat 200,000 houses in Paris, France.

The earth is an energy store, for the core of the earth is so hot that it is composed of molten rock. This rock is still cooling from the time the earth was created millions of years ago. This heat energy is known as geothermal energy. It can be captured and converted to provide a useful amount of energy. By drilling pipes deep into the hot rock, water can be pumped down into the rock. The water is then allowed to heat up before being pumped back to the surface. The hot water can be used directly for heating homes or can be used to drive steam turbines and generate electricity.

This geothermal plant in Iceland uses heat energy stored deep in the ground.

Key words
Battery a device that contains stored chemical energy that can be used to produce an electric current.
Fossil fuel a type of fuel made from the remains of plants and animals that died millions of years ago.
Hibernation a deep winter sleep that enables certain animals to survive cold winters.

Engines

Engines are machines that are designed to change one form of energy into another, especially kinetic energy. Most people think that engines are something human-made, but living organisms can be thought of as engines too. Our bodies are engines that convert food energy into other forms of energy, including kinetic energy.

Most human-made engines rely on combustion (the burning of a substance such as a fuel in oxygen) to release energy. The fuel molecules contain many chemical bonds that release considerable energy when they are broken and new bonds formed. Combustion also takes place in living organisms, though on a much smaller scale. All organisms, including humans, burn chemical substances such as sugar. When the bonds of the sugar are broken, energy is released. The combustion process has to be carefully controlled by enzymes, for a large release of energy would damage the organism's cell.

As a car travels along a road, its engine converts chemical energy into movement energy. The woman riding the bicycle is also an engine. Her body converts chemical energy into movement energy, which is used to turn the bicycle wheels.

Human-made engines

Most human-made engines are designed to turn the chemical energy contained within fuel into kinetic energy. For example, car engines convert the heat energy produced from burning fuel into kinetic energy to move the wheels. The fuel is normally mixed with air that contains oxygen and burned in closed cylinders inside the engine. This type of engine, called an internal combustion engine, is used in most road vehicles and some aircraft.

The internal combustion engine works by creating a series of controlled explosions. The engine is made of two parts bolted together: the cylinder head, which contains the combustion chambers and the camshaft, and the cylinder block, which contains the crankshaft. In a car engine, the gasoline and air are mixed in a carburetor and drawn into a combustion chamber at the top of each cylinder. The camshaft controls the opening and closing of the inlet and outlet valves, which draw the gasoline and air mixture into the chamber and vent the exhaust gases. These engines work on a four-stroke pattern (see diagram on page 41).

The piston is connected to the crankshaft with steel rods, and the crankshaft is linked to the wheels or propeller with a

How a four-stroke combustion engine works

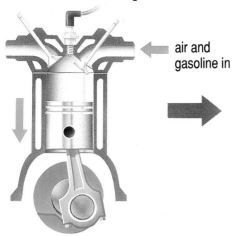

air and gasoline in

1 Fuel intake: the piston moves down, the inlet valves open and gasoline and air are drawn into the cylinder.

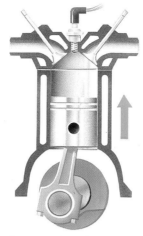

2 Compression: the valves are closed, the piston rises and compresses the mixture.

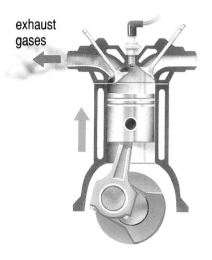

exhaust gases

4 Exhaust: the exhaust outlet opens and the piston rises again to expel gases.

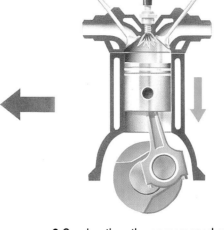

3 Combustion: the compressed gas is ignited by a spark from the spark plug and the piston is forced down by expanding gases.

transmission. As the pistons move down, the crankshaft is forced to rotate and this pushes the wheel around or spins the propeller.

Diesel engines also use a four-stroke pattern, but they burn diesel oil rather than gasoline. Diesel engines also differ from gasoline engines in that they do not use spark plugs. Instead, the diesel oil is squirted straight into the cylinders where it ignites as soon as it is mixed with air and is compressed.

One of the most important features of combustion engines is that they are not very efficient. Only a small amount of the chemical energy contained in oil or gasoline is converted into useful kinetic energy. The rest is wasted as heat energy. Combustion engines are particularly inefficient at low speeds. They also need a clutch and transmission to work efficiently and they produce many atmospheric pollutants in their exhaust. An alternative is the electric motor. Electric motors are quiet, work well at low speeds and do not produce pollution directly from the exhaust. However, they need a source of electricity to operate, and the batteries currently available are very heavy and cannot store nearly as much energy as a tank of gasoline or diesel fuel. Hence the range of these vehicles is limited. However, they may prove to be very useful to drive around cities.

Electric cars do not produce as much pollution as gasoline-powered cars, but the battery takes up a lot of space and is very heavy.

Electric engines

A simple electric motor
When the battery is connected, an electric current flows through the coil of wire. The current produces a force that turns the coil and the wooden block.

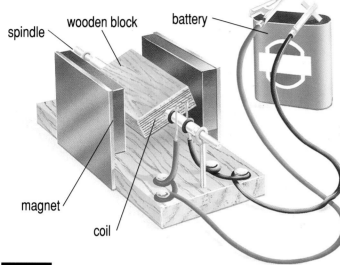

spindle
wooden block
battery
magnet
coil

? *What do all engines, including ourselves, have in common?*

An electric current produces a magnetic field. If a wire is placed within the magnetic field of a magnet and a current is passed along the wire, both the wire and magnet will try to move apart. This movement is called the motor effect and it is used in all electric motors, from the tiniest toys to the largest electric vehicles.

In a small electric motor, the wire is coiled so that a much greater length of wire can be held in the magnetic field and more force produced. The wire is often wound around a piece of soft iron, which turns the wire coil itself into an electromagnet. Most motors have more than one coil. The spinning electromagnets within the motor have contacts, called brushes, at each end of the coil so that the electric current can be passed to and from the spinning coil. An electric motor and a dynamo are very similar, for both consist of a coil surrounded by magnets. In a motor, however, the spinning coil is moved by electricity, while in the dynamo the spinning coil produces electricity.

Natural engines

One natural engine that produces very little pollution is the human body. It is quiet, works well at low speeds and uses renewable fuel. However, it cannot move very heavy loads and it gets tired easily!

Respiration in a cell

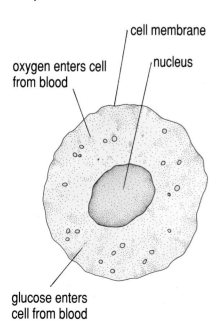

cell membrane
oxygen enters cell from blood
nucleus
glucose enters cell from blood

Every cell in our body, and those in other organisms, can be likened to an engine. Animals eat food to supply their body with a source of chemical energy that is then "burned" and converted to other forms of energy. In a large organism, such as a mammal, the food has to be chewed and swallowed. Once in the gut, it is digested and the soluble food absorbed into the body. For example, starches are digested into glucose. The glucose is absorbed into the blood stream and moved around the body to wherever it is required, especially the liver and the muscles. Once in the cells, the energy within the glucose is released in a process called respiration. This process involves breaking the glucose down into smaller molecules. Glucose is made up of many atoms bonded together. When the glucose is broken down, the energy that is contained in the bonds is released. The process of respiration is carried out in a series of tiny steps, so only a small amount of energy is released at a time. If all the energy contained within glucose was released at once, the cells would not be able to use it all at that time, and the unused energy would be wasted.

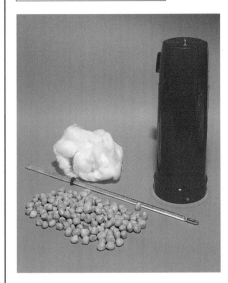

Respiration and heat energy

In this experiment you will show that respiration releases a lot of heat energy. You will need a small thermos, sterile cotton, a long thermometer and 200 g (7 oz.) of dried peas.

1 Soak the peas for a day in enough water to cover them so that they begin to germinate.

2 Half-fill the thermos with peas. Place a piece of cotton in the neck of the thermos.

3 Gently push the thermometer into the middle of the thermos and note the temperature. Remove the thermometer.

4 Support the thermos thermos upside down and leave for a week. (Heat rises so by placing the flask upside down heat cannot escape). Take another temperature reading.

Germinating pea seeds need energy for growth, so the stores of fat and starch in the seed are respired. However, heat energy is also released by the respiration process. A thermos is used so that any heat released by the seeds cannot escape.

There are two types of respiration. One type uses oxygen and is called aerobic respiration while the other, which does not require oxygen, is called anaerobic respiration. Humans respire aerobically most of the time but can respire anaerobically for very short periods.

Which organs of your body release each of the following—sound energy, kinetic energy and heat energy?

During a sprint, an athlete may not breathe in enough oxygen. The athlete takes deep breaths after the race to pay off the oxygen "debt." When yeast cells (inset) respire anaerobically, they produce alcohol and carbon dioxide.

Key words
Combustion a process that releases energy when a chemical is burned in air.
Respiration a process that releases energy from foods such as glucose in living cells.

Our garbage could be a source of energy in the future.

The future

Fossil fuels represent millions of years of stored sunshine. They are our most convenient source of stored energy, but they are being used up far faster than the rate at which they are being formed. They will eventually run out. It is important that alternative fuels and other energy sources are investigated. In the near future, more cars may run on alternatives to gasoline such as LPG (liquefied petroleum gas) and hydrogen. Power stations, too, may burn a wider range of fuels than they do at present. These might include animal slurry (similar to sewage), peat, domestic refuse and oil from shale.

Nuclear power is produced not by burning a fuel but by splitting an atom of uranium. Neutrons are fired at uranium atoms. When this happens the protons and the neutrons within the nucleus of the uranium atom split apart, releasing more neutrons and heat energy. These neutrons bump into other uranium atoms to set off a chain reaction. By carefully controlling these reactions a continuous supply of heat energy can be produced. Unfortunately, nuclear energy has many problems; not the least of which is that it is expensive and produces radioactive waste materials that are both long-lived and harmful to life. An alternative nuclear reaction, known as nuclear fusion, has recently been developed. In this reaction two different types of atom are fused together to form a new molecule. This takes place at an extremely high temperature and pressure, and heat energy is

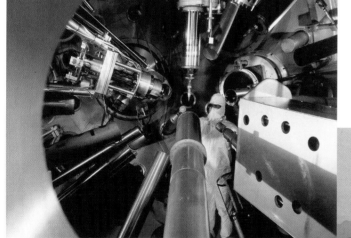

Today's nuclear power stations rely on nuclear fission to provide their energy (right). Nuclear fusion technology may replace this in the future. The Nova laser is used to start a nuclear fusion reaction (above).

released. Nuclear fusion is still a very new technology, and much more research is needed to make it commercially viable. This may take as long as 50 years, but it promises to be a clean energy source with no radioactive waste.

New types of battery are being designed for the electric motors that are used in the latest electric cars. These batteries contain sodium and sulfur rather than lead-acid, so they give greater range. Prototypes of the new battery enabled a new world distance record to be set for an electric vehicle—340 miles without recharging. The safety aspects of these batteries are critical, however, for both sodium and sulphur are highly reactive chemicals, making them potentially dangerous. Scientists are also working on the design of a molecular battery—a battery that will trap light rather like chlorophyll.

The arctic avens is a small plant with a yellow cup-shaped flower that is found in the Arctic. The shape of the flower is designed to reflect heat from sunlight into the middle of the flower where the reproductive organs are located. This heat raises the temperature in the middle of the flower by 10 °C (18°F). The flower also tracks the sun as it moves across the sky during the day, making sure that as much sunlight as possible falls on the petals. Similarities can be seen between the design of this flower and that of the latest solar water heaters. These solar heaters have parabolic (cup-shaped) mirrors that focus sunlight on to a narrow collector. A motor in the heater enables the mirror to track the sun. These refinements mean that this solar heater has a 70 percent efficiency rate in its energy conversion—much higher than conventional solar panels.

Energy is essential to life as we know it. Although our energy demands are ever increasing, the supply of fossil fuels on which we depend will soon be exhausted. All of the technologies just described, and others besides, will need to be harnessed for us to continue to lead an energy-hungry lifestyle.

The flower of the arctic avens is cup-shaped so that heat energy in sunlight is reflected into the middle of the flower. The latest designs of solar heater use the same shape.

Glossary

artery blood vessel carrying blood away from the heart.

biomass plant materials and animal waste used as a source of fuel.

ceramic a material made of clay and fired in a kiln.

chlorophyll green pigment in plants.

coppicing cutting tree trunks at ground level and allowing the shoots to regrow

density the mass of something divided by its volume.

electron a negatively charged particle found in a "cloud" around the nucleus of an atom.

enzyme natural catalyst that begins a reaction or increases the rate of the reaction in cells.

geothermal heat from the ground.

hypothermia a condition in which the body temperature falls below 35°C (95°F).

neutron an uncharged particle found in the nucleus of an atom.

oxidation a reaction in which an element or compound combines with oxygen or loses electrons.

protein a large molecule made of amino acids found in living organisms.

proton a positively charged particle found in the nucleus of an atom.

reservoir a large store of water, usually in the form of a lake.

semiconductor a material that only partially conducts electricity.

static electricity form of electricity that does not move, created by an attraction between charged objects.

vein a blood vessel that carries blood back to the heart.

Answers to the questions

p. 9 Food would cook more quickly in metal dish since metal better conductor of heat than glass.

p. 9 You feel a draft because a strongly burning fire heats up air, which rises, and cold air moves in at the bottom of the fire to replace hot, rising air.

p.11 Marathon runners—"space blankets" reduce heat losses from the runners so they keep warm and do not lose too much heat energy.

p.11 White houses—white reflects heat energy, keeping house cool in summer.

p.13 Arctic summers are warm, and the animal cannot lose heat easily because of its excellent insulation.

p.15 Cover hot water tank and hot pipes, double glazing, cavity wall insulation.

p.18 Enzymes work best at approx. 35–40°C (95–104°F), very high temperatures destroy them.

p.19 Rubbing alcohol needs heat energy to evaporate, so it takes heat energy from the skin, which then feels cooler.

p.20 Water vapor in the air condenses directly into ice when it touches the cold glass.

p.23 Parasitic plants produce "suckers" that penetrate the host plant and withdraw food such as sucrose.

p.29 Potential energy to kinetic energy to electrical energy.

p.33 Food chains—number of links limited by the huge energy losses at each stage since only 1–20 percent of the energy will be transferred to the next animal in the chain.

p.36 Heat comes from the respiration of the millions of bacteria, fungi and small animals feeding on the decaying material in the compost heap.

p.34 The trees would use carbon dioxide in photosynthesis and this would help to reduce the levels of carbon dioxide in the atmosphere.

p.38 Pasta, rice, bread, cookies, onions, potatoes, cereals, etc.

p.42 Engines do work, transform energy usually chemical energy into kinetic and heat energy, need a fuel.

p.43 Sound—larynx, heart; kinetic—heart; heat—liver.

Index

Main topics appear in **bold face** type.